STEPHEN HAWKING

LEGENDS AND LEGACIES

THE BIOGRAPHY OF
STEPHEN HAWKING

Published by
Rupa Publications India Pvt. Ltd 2024
7/16, Ansari Road, Daryaganj
New Delhi 110002

Sales centres:
Bengaluru Chennai
Hyderabad Jaipur Kathmandu
Kolkata Mumbai Prayagraj

Copyright © Rupa Publications India Pvt. Ltd 2024

The views and opinions expressed in this book are the author's own and the facts are as reported by him which have been verified to the extent possible, and the publishers are not in any way liable for the same.

All rights reserved.
No part of this publication may be reproduced, transmitted, or stored in a retrieval system, in any form or by any means, electronic, mechanical, photocopying, recording or otherwise, without the prior permission of the publisher.

P-ISBN: 978-93-6156-822-0
E-ISBN: 978-93-6156-225-9

First impression 2024

10 9 8 7 6 5 4 3 2 1

Printed in India

This book is sold subject to the condition that it shall not, by way of trade or otherwise, be lent, resold, hired out, or otherwise circulated, without the publisher's prior consent, in any form of binding or cover other than that in which it is published.

Contents

Introduction	7
Early Life and Education (1942-1965)	9
The Onset of ALS and Early Career (1963-1975)	14
Breakthroughs and Rising Fame (1975-1988)	20
Scientific Contributions and Later Career (1988-2018)	26
Personal Life and Challenges	31
Legacy and Impact	35
Public Engagement and Media Presence	42
Philosophical Views and Public Opinions	46
Technological Innovations and Adaptations	50
Research Collaborations and International Influence	54
Personal Philosophies and Beliefs	59
Influence on Arts and Culture	63
Future Visions and Predictions	67
Educational Initiatives and Foundations	70
Personal Anecdotes and Memorable Stories	74
Conclusion	77
Motivational Quotes From Stephen Hawking	79

Introduction

Stephen Hawking is a name known worldwide, not just for his incredible discoveries in science but also for his inspiring life story. He showed us that we can still achieve great things even when faced with big challenges. Hawking made important contributions to our understanding of the universe, especially about black holes and the origins of the cosmos. His work has changed the way scientists think about these topics and has inspired many people to learn more about science.

Hawking's most famous discovery is something called Hawking radiation. This is the idea that black holes, which were once thought to swallow everything and never let anything escape, actually give off a tiny bit of radiation. This was a huge surprise to scientists, making them rethink what they knew about black holes. It also connected two big ideas in physics: general relativity, which explains how gravity works, and quantum mechanics, which explains the behaviour of tiny particles.

Besides his scientific work, Stephen Hawking became a well-known author. His book "A Brief History of Time" was written for people who aren't scientists but are curious about how the universe works. It became a best-seller and helped millions of people simply understand complex ideas. Hawking had a special talent for explaining difficult concepts so that everyone could understand them.

Hawking's personal story is just as remarkable as his scientific achievements. When he was 21 years old, he was diagnosed with a disease called amyotrophic lateral sclerosis (ALS), which gradually paralyzed him. Doctors told him he had only a few years to live, but he defied the odds and continued to work and live for more than 50 years. Despite his physical limitations, he communicated using a speech-generating device and continued to share his ideas with the world.

Stephen Hawking also became a familiar face in popular culture. He appeared on TV shows like "The Simpsons," "Star Trek: The Next Generation," and "The Big Bang Theory," which helped make science fun and interesting for many people. His life was also the subject of a movie called "The Theory of Everything," which showed how he overcame his illness to make important scientific discoveries.

Stephen Hawking's life and work teach us many valuable lessons. He showed us that curiosity and determination can lead to amazing discoveries, even in the face of great challenges. His contributions to science have changed how we understand the universe, and his story continues to inspire people all over the world. As we learn more about his life, we can see how his passion for understanding the universe and his unbreakable spirit made him one of the most remarkable figures in modern history.

1

Early Life and Education (1942-1965)

Birth and Family Background

Stephen William Hawking was born on January 8, 1942, in Oxford, England, during World War II. His parents, Frank and Isobel Hawking, were both highly educated and valued knowledge and learning. Frank, a medical researcher specializing in tropical diseases, and Isobel, a political activist and former secretary, fostered a home environment where curiosity and intellectual pursuits were encouraged. The Hawking family lived modestly, but their home was always filled with books and stimulating discussions.

Stephen was the eldest of four children. His siblings, Mary, Philippa, and Edward, each had their own talents and interests, but it was Stephen who showed an early fascination with how things worked. The family often discussed current events and scientific ideas over dinner, nurturing Stephen's budding interest in the world around him.

> **Fun Fact**
> Stephen Hawking was born exactly 300 years after the death of Galileo Galilei, another famous scientist.

Childhood in London and St. Albans

Stephen spent his early years in London. The aftermath of World War II meant that resources were scarce, and the city was recovering from the devastation of the war. In 1950, when Stephen was eight years old, the family moved to St. Albans, a historic market town north of London, in search of better educational opportunities and a more peaceful environment.

In St. Albans, Stephen attended the prestigious St. Albans School. Here, his intellectual abilities began to shine. Although not always the top of his class, Stephen was known for his quick wit and deep thinking. He loved reading science fiction and playing with his homemade inventions, which ranged from model airplanes to complex board games he designed himself.

Fun Fact
The Hawkings' house was so crowded with books that they used the stairs as extra bookshelves!

His natural curiosity led him to explore a wide range of subjects, but he was particularly drawn to mathematics and physics.

Stephen's father wanted him to follow a career in medicine, but Stephen was more interested in understanding the fundamental laws that govern the universe.

Early Education and Interests

At St. Albans School, Stephen's talents started to get noticed. His teachers recognized his exceptional ability to grasp complex mathematical concepts, even though he sometimes appeared disinterested in the routine of schoolwork. Stephen preferred self-study and solving problems in his own unique way. He enjoyed extracurricular activities such as debating and joining the school's science club, where he could indulge his passion for understanding how things worked.

> **Fun Fact**
> Stephen and his friends built a computer out of old clock parts, telephone switchboards, and other recycled items.

Outside of school, Stephen was an active and curious child. He was involved in various hobbies, including hiking, rowing, and experimenting with electronics. His inquisitive nature was evident in his projects, such as building a model train set that ran through his family's garden. His interest in the mechanics of the universe only grew stronger over time.

Undergraduate Years at Oxford University

In 1959, at the age of 17, Stephen won a scholarship to University College, Oxford, where he decided to study physics, a subject that combined his love for mathematics with his fascination with the universe. At Oxford, Stephen found the academic work relatively easy and spent much of his time socializing and participating in activities like rowing. Despite his laid-back approach to studying, his natural brilliance shone through.

> **Fun Fact**
> Stephen once calculated that he studied for only about an hour a day while at Oxford!

Stephen's time at Oxford was formative. He enjoyed the freedom to explore his interests and engage with other bright minds. He developed a reputation for his wit and sense of humour, often playing practical jokes on his friends. Despite his casual attitude towards his coursework, he graduated with a first-class honors degree in natural science, specializing in physics, in 1962.

Graduate Studies at Cambridge University

After completing his undergraduate degree, Stephen chose to pursue graduate studies at Trinity Hall, Cambridge, focusing on cosmology, a relatively new field that sought to understand the origins and structure of the universe. His decision was influenced by the work of Dennis Sciama, one of the leading physicists of the time, who became Stephen's mentor.

However, during his first year at Cambridge, Stephen began to notice symptoms of physical weakness and clumsiness. After a series of tests, he was diagnosed with amyotrophic lateral sclerosis (ALS), a rare and progressive neurodegenerative disease. Doctors gave him a prognosis of only a few years to live. This devastating news could have easily derailed his academic career, but it had the opposite effect on Stephen. Determined to make the most of his time, he threw himself into his work with renewed vigor.

Despite the challenges posed by his illness, Stephen's work at Cambridge flourished. He focused on the properties of black holes and the origins of the universe, topics that would later become central to his career. His early research contributed significantly to our understanding of singularities and the Big Bang theory, laying the groundwork for many of his later discoveries.

> **Fun Fact**
> Stephen met his future wife, Jane Wilde, at a New Year's party just before he was diagnosed with ALS.

In summary, Stephen Hawking's early life and education were characterized by a blend of intellectual curiosity, resilience, and determination. From his early days in St. Albans, through his time at Oxford and Cambridge, Stephen's passion for understanding the universe drove him to overcome immense personal challenges. His early achievements set the stage for a career that would profoundly impact our understanding of the cosmos.

2
The Onset of ALS and Early Career (1963-1975)

Diagnosis with Amyotrophic Lateral Sclerosis (ALS)

In the early 1960s, while Stephen Hawking was pursuing his graduate studies at Cambridge University, he began to experience unusual physical symptoms. He noticed that he was becoming increasingly clumsy and prone to tripping and falling. His speech also started to slur slightly. Initially, Stephen dismissed these symptoms as the result of his natural awkwardness, but as they persisted, he sought medical advice.

In 1963, after a series of tests and medical consultations, Stephen was diagnosed with amyotrophic lateral sclerosis (ALS), also known as Lou Gehrig's disease. ALS is a progressive neurodegenerative disease that affects nerve cells in the brain and spinal cord, leading to the loss of muscle control. The diagnosis was devastating. At the time, doctors gave him a life expectancy of just two to three years. The news was a severe blow to the young scientist, who was only 21 years old and just beginning to make his mark in the field of physics.

> **Fun Fact**
> Despite his grim prognosis, Stephen Hawking lived for more than 50 years after his diagnosis, defying all medical expectations.

Coping with the Disease and Its Impact on His Life and Career

The diagnosis of ALS was a severe blow to Stephen, who was only 21 years old and had just embarked on his career in physics. Initially, he fell into a deep depression, feeling that his future had been stripped away. However, the support of his family, friends, and especially his future wife, Jane Wilde, played a crucial role in helping him cope with his new reality. Jane's optimism and belief in Stephen's abilities were instrumental in lifting his spirits and encouraging him to continue his work.

Determined not to let the disease define him, Stephen returned to his studies with renewed focus and determination. He began using a wheelchair as his mobility declined and later relied on a speech-generating device to communicate. These adaptations allowed him to continue his research and academic pursuits despite his physical limitations.

> **Fun Fact**
> Stephen once joked that one of the benefits of his condition was that it freed him from distractions, allowing him to concentrate entirely on his work.

Stephen's sense of humour and his ability to stay positive in the face of adversity became well-known. He often used humour to cope with the difficulties posed by his illness, which endeared him to colleagues and friends. His perseverance and ability to continue his work despite his physical challenges served as an inspiration to many.

Marriage to Jane Wilde

In 1965, Stephen married Jane Wilde, a fellow student he had met shortly before his diagnosis. Jane was a language student and shared Stephen's love of learning. Their relationship provided Stephen with emotional stability and support during a challenging time in his life. Jane's unwavering belief in Stephen's potential and her practical support were vital in helping him to continue his academic work.

Jane and Stephen's marriage was filled with both joy and challenges. They had three children: Robert, born in 1967; Lucy, born in 1970; and Timothy, born in 1979. Despite the challenges posed by Stephen's illness, the family led a relatively normal life, with Jane managing most of the household responsibilities while Stephen focused on his research.

> **Fun Fact**
> Jane and Stephen's wedding took place just a week before Stephen's 23rd birthday.

Their partnership was a remarkable example of resilience and mutual support. Jane's dedication allowed Stephen to continue his groundbreaking work, and she played a crucial role in helping him navigate the difficulties of living with ALS. Their marriage was not without its struggles, but their shared commitment to Stephen's work and their family life was unwavering.

Early Academic Appointments and Research Work

Despite the progression of his disease, Stephen continued to make significant strides in his academic career. In 1966, he completed his doctoral thesis, which explored the implications and consequences of the expanding universe. His thesis earned him a research fellowship at Gonville and Caius College, Cambridge, providing him with the opportunity to continue his research.

Stephen's early research focused on singularities, regions in space where the density of matter becomes infinite, such as those found at the center of black holes. His work in this area led to groundbreaking discoveries and new insights into the nature of the universe. He collaborated with renowned mathematician Roger Penrose, and together they developed new theories about singularities, providing key insights into the conditions of the early universe.

> **Fun Fact**
> Stephen's doctoral thesis was so influential that it crashed the University of Cambridge's website when it was made publicly available online in 2017, due to the high number of people wanting to read it.

During this period, Stephen also began to establish himself as a leading voice in the field of cosmology. His work on singularities and black holes challenged existing ideas and opened up new areas of research. He quickly gained a reputation for his innovative thinking and his ability to tackle some of the most challenging problems in theoretical physics.

Development of Initial Theories on Black Holes and Singularities

One of Stephen's most significant early contributions to theoretical physics was his work on black holes. In collaboration with mathematician Roger Penrose, Stephen developed new ideas about the nature of singularities. Their work showed that if general relativity is correct, then the universe must have begun as a singularity, a point where space and time are infinitely curved.

In the early 1970s, Stephen proposed the revolutionary theory that black holes are not entirely black. Instead, they emit radiation due to quantum effects near the event horizon, the boundary beyond which nothing can escape. This radiation, now known as Hawking radiation, was a groundbreaking discovery that combined principles of quantum mechanics and general relativity, two major fields in physics.

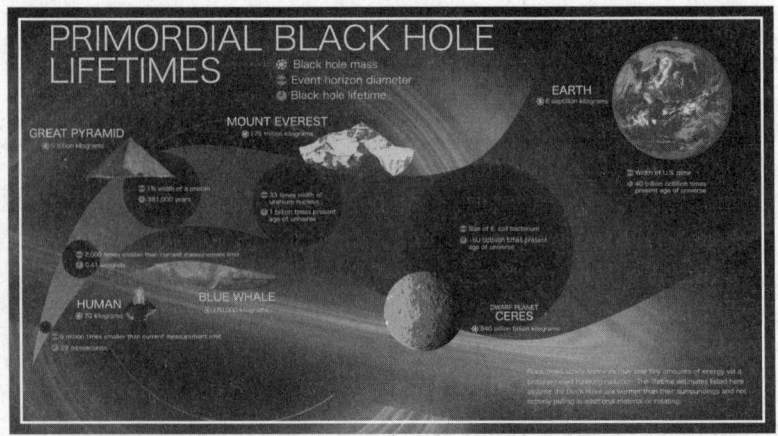

> **Fun Fact**
> The theoretical concept of Hawking radiation suggests that black holes can eventually evaporate and disappear over time, which was a radical idea when first proposed.

Stephen's theories on black holes and singularities not only advanced our understanding of these mysterious objects but also opened new avenues of research in theoretical physics. His work laid the foundation for many future discoveries and established him as a leading figure in the field.

Continued Research and Growing Reputation

As Stephen's career progressed, he continued to build on his early work, developing new theories and refining existing ones. His research was characterized by a willingness to explore bold ideas and challenge established thinking. This approach earned him both respect and admiration from his peers.

Throughout the 1970s, Stephen's work on black holes and the early universe garnered widespread attention. He published several influential papers and began to receive invitations to speak at conferences and universities around the world. His ability to explain complex scientific concepts in an accessible way made him a popular speaker and helped to raise public awareness of his work.

By the mid-1970s, Stephen had become one of the most prominent and respected physicists of his generation. His contributions to the field of cosmology had established him as a leading authority on black holes and the origins of the universe. His resilience in the face of ALS, combined with his groundbreaking research, made him an inspirational figure both within and outside the scientific community.

> **Fun Fact**
> Despite his physical limitations, Stephen loved to travel and often attended conferences and speaking engagements around the world.

3
Breakthroughs and Rising Fame (1975-1988)

Hawking's Key Contributions to Cosmology and Theoretical Physics

During the period from 1975 to 1988, Stephen Hawking made several groundbreaking contributions to the fields of cosmology and theoretical physics. His work during these years significantly advanced our understanding of the universe and cemented his reputation as one of the most brilliant minds in science.

Hawking's research focused on the nature of black holes, the origins of the universe, and the interplay between quantum mechanics and general relativity. His early work on singularities with Roger Penrose had already established him as a leading figure in theoretical physics. Building on this foundation, Hawking continued to explore some of the most fundamental questions about the cosmos.

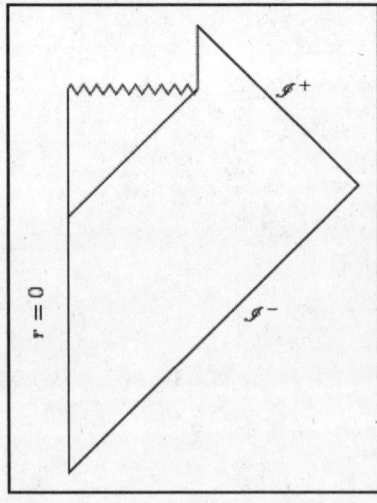

In the mid-1970s, Hawking developed the four laws of black hole mechanics, which parallel the laws of thermodynamics.

This framework was pivotal in the theoretical understanding of black holes and their behaviour. These laws described how black holes interact with the rest of the universe, particularly focusing on their mass, area, spin, and charge.

Discovery of Hawking Radiation

One of Stephen Hawking's most famous contributions to science is the theoretical prediction of Hawking radiation. In the mid-1970s, Hawking proposed that black holes are not entirely black but instead emit radiation due to quantum effects near the event horizon. This groundbreaking theory challenged the previously held belief that nothing could escape from a black hole.

Hawking's insight was that pairs of virtual particles are constantly being created and annihilated in space. Near the event horizon of a black hole, one of these particles could fall into the black hole while the other escapes, effectively causing the black hole to lose mass and emit radiation. This radiation, now known as Hawking radiation, suggested that black holes could eventually evaporate and disappear over time.

The discovery of Hawking radiation had profound implications for our understanding of black holes and the fundamental laws of physics. It suggested that black holes could have a finite lifespan and that information might not be lost when an object falls into a black hole, a topic that continues to be a subject of intense research and debate.

Hawking's work on black holes and radiation also led him to explore the nature of the universe's beginning and its ultimate fate. He proposed that the Big Bang, the event that marked the origin of the universe, was similar to

> **Fun Fact**
> Hawking radiation is a concept that combines principles from both quantum mechanics and general relativity, two areas of physics that are typically difficult to reconcile.

a black hole in reverse. This idea helped to link the study of the universe's inception with the study of black holes, providing a more comprehensive understanding of cosmology.

Publication of "A Brief History of Time" and Its Impact

In 1988, Stephen Hawking published "A Brief History of Time: From the Big Bang to Black Holes." The book aimed to explain complex scientific concepts in cosmology and theoretical physics to a general audience. Hawking wanted to make the wonders of the universe accessible to people without a background in science.

"A Brief History of Time" quickly became a bestseller, selling millions of copies worldwide and being translated into numerous languages. The book covered topics such as the nature of time, the Big Bang, black holes, and the search for a unified theory of physics. Hawking's ability to explain intricate ideas clearly and engagingly captivated readers and sparked widespread interest in cosmology.

The success of the book not only brought Stephen Hawking widespread recognition but also helped to popularize science. It inspired many people to learn more about the universe and consider careers in scientific fields. The book's impact extended beyond the scientific community, making Hawking a household name and an influential figure in popular culture.

> **Fun Fact**
> "A Brief History of Time" spent more than four years on the London Sunday Times bestseller list.

In "A Brief History of Time," Hawking tackled some of the most profound questions about the universe. He discussed the nature of time, explaining how it might flow differently in different circumstances and how it could have begun with the Big Bang. He also delved into the concept of the "no-boundary condition," suggesting that the universe may be finite but without boundaries, akin to the surface of a sphere.

The book's success also demonstrated the public's appetite for knowledge about the cosmos. It bridged the gap between complex scientific theories and the general public, making science more approachable and exciting. Hawking's ability to simplify and convey deep scientific ideas understandably was a key factor in the book's widespread appeal.

> **Fun Fact**
> Stephen Hawking made several guest appearances on popular TV shows, including "The Simpsons" and "Star Trek: The Next Generation."

Hawking's Growing Fame and Public Recognition

As Hawking's scientific achievements and the success of "A Brief History of Time" brought him increasing fame, he became one of the most recognizable scientists in the world. Despite his physical limitations due to ALS, Hawking's wit, charisma, and intellect made him a compelling public figure.

Hawking's growing fame led to numerous accolades and awards. He was elected a Fellow of the Royal Society (FRS) in 1974 and later became the Lucasian Professor of Mathematics at Cambridge University, a position once held by Sir Isaac Newton. In 1982, he was made a Commander of the Order of the British Empire (CBE) for his contributions to science.

Hawking's public recognition extended beyond

the scientific community. He appeared in documentaries, gave interviews, and participated in various public speaking engagements. His life and work were celebrated in the media, and he became an inspirational figure for people around the world, demonstrating the power of the human spirit and the pursuit of knowledge.

Hawking's rise to fame also highlighted the importance of making science accessible to the public. His ability to communicate complex ideas in a way that was both understandable and fascinating helped bridge the gap between the scientific community and the general public. Hawking's influence extended to popular culture, where his unique voice and iconic status made him a beloved figure.

Continued Research and Influence

During this period, Hawking continued to push the boundaries of theoretical physics. He worked on various projects, including the quest for a unified theory that could reconcile general relativity and quantum mechanics. His research contributed to the development of new ideas and theories that continue to shape our understanding of the universe.

Hawking's contributions to science were not limited to his own research. He mentored and collaborated with other scientists, fostering an environment of intellectual curiosity and innovation. His work inspired a new generation of physicists and cosmologists, many of whom continued to build on his groundbreaking theories.

As Stephen Hawking's fame and influence grew, he used his platform to advocate for

> **Fun Fact**
> Hawking's voice synthesizer became an integral part of his identity, even though it had an American accent. He chose to keep it because it was how people recognized him.

important causes. He spoke out on issues such as climate change, nuclear disarmament, and the importance of scientific research. His public statements often carried significant weight due to his status as a leading scientist and his personal story of overcoming adversity.

Hawking's role as a public intellectual expanded during these years. He participated in public debates and discussions, often emphasizing the importance of science education and the need for society to address global challenges through scientific understanding and innovation. His ability to engage with the public on critical issues demonstrated the broader impact of his work beyond theoretical physics.

> **Fun Fact**
> - Despite his busy schedule, Hawking enjoyed leisure activities like playing chess and watching science fiction movies, which provided him with relaxation and inspiration.

By 1988, Stephen Hawking had firmly established himself as one of the most influential scientists of the 20th century. His key contributions to cosmology and theoretical physics, combined with his ability to communicate complex ideas to the public, made him a beloved and inspirational figure. His work not only advanced our understanding of the universe but also inspired millions to look up at the stars and wonder about the mysteries of the cosmos.

Hawking's achievements during this period were marked by a relentless pursuit of knowledge and an unwavering commitment to his research. His breakthroughs in black hole theory, his popularization of science through "A Brief History of Time," and his public engagement all contributed to his lasting legacy. Stephen Hawking's journey from a young physicist facing a life-threatening illness to a world-renowned scientist and public figure is a testament to his extraordinary intellect, resilience, and passion for discovery.

4
Scientific Contributions and Later Career (1988-2018)

Further Work on Black Holes, the Nature of the Universe, and the Theory of Everything

From 1988 to 2018, Stephen Hawking continued to make significant contributions to theoretical physics and cosmology. His work during this period furthered our understanding of black holes, the nature of the universe, and the quest for a unified theory of physics.

Hawking's research in these years delved deeper into the enigmatic realm of black holes. Building upon his earlier insights, he explored the subtleties of black hole thermodynamics and the behaviour of information within them. His investigations into the information paradox, concerning the apparent loss of information in black holes, led to the proposal of various solutions that challenged conventional notions of spacetime and quantum mechanics.

In addition to his pioneering work on black holes, Hawking continued to unravel the mysteries of the universe's origins and structure. He collaborated with fellow physicists on theories of cosmic inflation and the multiverse, offering new perspectives on the fundamental laws governing our universe and its place within a broader cosmological framework.

Collaborative Projects and Influential Publications

Throughout his later career, Stephen Hawking collaborated with numerous scientists and continued to publish influential papers. His collaborative efforts brought together some of the brightest minds in physics to tackle complex problems and explore new ideas.

One notable collaboration was with physicist Thomas Hertog, with whom Hawking worked on the theory of cosmic inflation and the multiverse. Their research proposed that the universe's beginning was determined by the laws of quantum mechanics, leading to the possibility of multiple universes with different physical laws.

Hawking also co-authored several papers on the information paradox with other leading physicists. These papers explored various solutions to the paradox, including the idea that information could be preserved in a "soft hair" on the event horizon of black holes, a concept that added new dimensions to the understanding of black hole mechanics.

In addition to his research papers, Hawking authored several books aimed at both scientific and general audiences. His publications included "The Universe in a Nutshell" (2001), which provided an accessible overview of modern theoretical physics, and "The Grand Design" (2010), co-written with Leonard Mlodinow, which discussed the latest theories about the universe's origins and the nature of reality.

> **Fun Fact**
>
> Hawking once challenged a Russian billionaire to a chess match while floating in zero gravity aboard a parabolic flight.
>
> Despite his physical limitations, Hawking traveled extensively, visiting countries around the world to give lectures and attend scientific conferences.

Roles at Cambridge and Other Academic Institutions

Stephen Hawking's academic career was closely associated with the University of Cambridge, where he held the position of Lucasian Professor of Mathematics from 1979 to 2009. This prestigious chair, once held by Sir Isaac Newton, provided Hawking with a platform to conduct his research and mentor the next generation of physicists.

Even after stepping down from the Lucasian Professorship, Hawking remained actively involved in academia. He continued to work at the Department of Applied Mathematics and Theoretical Physics (DAMTP) at Cambridge and held the title of Director of Research at the Centre for Theoretical Cosmology, which he helped establish.

> **Fun Fact**
> Hawking's iconic voice synthesizer, which he used to communicate, was originally sponsored by Intel, who later gave him the updated software for free.
> Despite his busy schedule, Hawking enjoyed attending scientific conferences and engaging with students and researchers from diverse backgrounds.

Hawking also held visiting positions at various institutions around the world, including Caltech in the United States and the Perimeter Institute for Theoretical Physics in Canada. These roles allowed him to collaborate with international researchers and contribute to global scientific discussions.

Public Lectures, Media Appearances, and Contributions to Science Communication

Stephen Hawking was not only a brilliant scientist but also a passionate communicator who believed in making science accessible to the public. He delivered numerous public lectures and participated in a variety of media appearances, helping to demystify complex scientific concepts and inspire curiosity about the universe.

Hawking's lectures were known for their clarity, humour, and ability to engage audiences of all ages. He used a speech-generating device to deliver his talks, often interspersing them with witty remarks and thought-provoking insights. His lectures covered a wide range of topics, from the nature of black holes to the potential future of humanity.

Hawking's media appearances included interviews on television and radio, as well as cameo roles in popular TV shows such as "The Simpsons," "Star Trek: The Next Generation," and "The Big Bang Theory." These appearances helped to humanize the scientist and brought his work to a broader audience.

In addition to his public engagements, Hawking was committed to science education. He supported initiatives aimed at promoting STEM (science, technology, engineering, and mathematics) education and encouraged young people to pursue careers in scientific fields. His outreach efforts included writing children's books with his daughter Lucy, such as "George's Secret Key to the Universe," which introduced young readers to fundamental concepts in physics and astronomy.

Hawking's contributions to science communication extended to his advocacy for the future of humanity. He spoke on issues such as climate change, artificial intelligence, and space exploration, emphasizing the need for global cooperation and scientific innovation to address these challenges. His insights into these topics were widely respected and often sparked important discussions among scientists, policymakers, and the public.

> **Fun Fact**
>
> Hawking once appeared in an episode of "The Big Bang Theory," where he played himself in a scene with Sheldon Cooper, who was seeking advice on his research.
>
> Despite his physical limitations, Hawking traveled extensively, visiting countries around the world to give lectures and attend scientific conferences.

Legacy and Influence

Stephen Hawking's later career was marked by a relentless pursuit of knowledge and a commitment to sharing that knowledge with the world. His scientific contributions, from his work on black holes and the nature of the universe to his exploration of the theory of everything, have left an indelible mark on the field of theoretical physics.

Hawking's ability to communicate complex ideas in an accessible and engaging manner helped to inspire a new generation of scientists and foster a greater appreciation for the wonders of the universe. His public lectures, media appearances, and advocacy for science education ensured that his influence extended far beyond the academic community.

By the time of his passing in 2018, Stephen Hawking had become a symbol of intellectual curiosity, resilience, and the power of the human spirit. His legacy continues to inspire scientists and laypeople alike, reminding us of the boundless possibilities that come with exploring the mysteries of the cosmos.

5
Personal Life and Challenges

Marriage and Family Life

Stephen Hawking's personal life was marked by profound relationships and familial support. In 1965, he married Jane Wilde, a friend from his college days. Their union brought three children: Robert, Lucy, and Timothy. Despite the challenges posed by Hawking's demanding career and health issues, the couple remained dedicated to each other and their family.

Their marriage was a testament to love and resilience, enduring through decades of triumphs and trials. Jane Wilde stood by Hawking's side through his battle with ALS, providing unwavering support and care. Despite the physical limitations

Fun Fact
Hawking's children, Robert and Lucy, followed in their father's footsteps by pursuing careers in science and academia, reflecting his influence and inspiration within his own family.

imposed by his condition, Hawking found solace and joy in the love of his family, cherishing moments spent together amidst the demands of his scientific pursuits.

Struggles with ALS and Reliance on Technology for Communication

In 1963, at the age of 21, Stephen Hawking was diagnosed with amyotrophic lateral sclerosis (ALS), a progressive neurodegenerative disease that eventually left him almost entirely paralyzed. Despite the devastating prognosis, Hawking continued his academic pursuits with determination and resilience.

Fun Fact
Hawking's iconic voice synthesizer was originally programmed to have an American accent, but he chose to keep it that way even after updates were available because it became part of his recognizable persona.

As the disease progressed, Hawking gradually lost control of his motor functions, including his ability to speak. He relied on a speech-generating device to communicate, using a sensor attached to his glasses to select words and phrases displayed on a screen. This technology became synonymous with his identity and played a crucial role in enabling him to continue his scientific work and engage with the world.

Hawking's reliance on technology for communication not only facilitated his scientific endeavors but also became a symbol of his indomitable spirit and determination to overcome adversity. Despite the physical limitations imposed by ALS, Hawking refused to be silenced, using his voice synthesizer to express his ideas and share his insights with the world.

Relationship with Jane Wilde and Subsequent Marriages

Hawking's marriage to Jane Wilde was marked by both love and challenges. Jane provided unwavering support to Hawking throughout their marriage, assisting him with everyday tasks and caring for him as his physical condition deteriorated. Their relationship faced strains due to the pressures of his illness and the demands of his career, leading to periods of tension and difficulty.

Despite their enduring bond, Stephen and Jane ultimately divorced in 1995 after nearly 30 years of marriage. Following their divorce, Hawking married Elaine Mason, one of his nurses. Their relationship was met with controversy and speculation, with some questioning the circumstances of their marriage. The union ended in divorce in 2006.

Fun Fact
Despite his busy schedule, Hawking enjoyed leisure activities like playing chess and watching science fiction movies, which provided him with relaxation and inspiration.

Balancing Personal Life with Professional Achievements

Throughout his life, Stephen Hawking faced the challenge of balancing his personal relationships with his professional achievements. Despite the demands of his career and the limitations imposed by his illness, he remained committed to his family and valued their support and companionship.

> **Fun Fact**
> Hawking was known for his sense of humour, often incorporating wit and playful banter into his interactions with colleagues, friends, and family, which helped to lighten the mood during difficult times.

Hawking's dedication to his work sometimes led to conflicts with his loved ones, as he devoted long hours to his research and academic pursuits. However, he also cherished moments spent with his children and grandchildren, finding joy in their company and shared experiences.

Scientific Information:

Despite his physical limitations, Hawking continued to make groundbreaking contributions to theoretical physics, including his work on black holes, quantum mechanics, and the nature of the universe. His research expanded our understanding of the cosmos and inspired new avenues of scientific inquiry.

Despite the challenges he faced in his personal life, Stephen Hawking's determination and resilience allowed him to navigate the complexities of relationships and continue his scientific endeavours with passion and purpose. His ability to overcome adversity and find meaning in both his professional and personal life remains an enduring aspect of his legacy.

6
Legacy and Impact

Stephen Hawking's influence on the world extended far beyond the confines of his groundbreaking scientific work. His contributions to science, his ability to overcome adversity, and his enduring presence in popular culture have left an indelible mark on the world. This chapter delves into the multifaceted legacy he left behind.

Hawking's Influence on Science and Popular Culture

Science: Stephen Hawking was a brilliant theoretical physicist whose work revolutionized our understanding of the universe. One of his most notable contributions was his work on black holes. In 1974, he proposed what is now known as "Hawking radiation," a theory suggesting that black holes are not entirely black but emit radiation and eventually evaporate over time. This groundbreaking idea combined principles from quantum mechanics, general relativity, and thermodynamics, and it fundamentally altered the way scientists understand black holes and the nature of the universe.

Hawking's work on black holes also led to significant insights into the nature of singularities, the points of infinite density at the center of black holes. His collaboration with mathematician Roger Penrose demonstrated that singularities are a common feature of general relativity, leading to profound implications for our understanding of space and time.

> **Fun Fact**
> Hawking's paper on black holes and Hawking radiation was initially so controversial that he had difficulty getting it published. Today, it's considered one of the most important papers in theoretical physics. Additionally, Hawking lost a famous bet with Kip Thorne about the nature of black holes, conceding that they do indeed exist as previously thought.

Popular Culture: Hawking's reach extended well beyond the academic world. He became a pop culture icon, featuring in numerous TV shows, movies, and even animated series. His distinctive computer-generated voice and sharp wit made him a beloved figure. For instance, he made memorable appearances on shows like "The Simpsons," "Star Trek: The Next Generation," and "The Big Bang Theory." These appearances helped to humanize science and bring complex ideas to a broader audience, showing that science could be both accessible and entertaining.

Hawking's Cameo in Music: Hawking's voice was featured in the Pink Floyd song "Keep Talking" from their 1994 album "The Division Bell." The inclusion of his synthesized speech added a unique touch to the song and highlighted his influence beyond the realm of science and television.

Contributions to Our Understanding of the Universe

Stephen Hawking's scientific contributions were numerous and profound, significantly advancing our knowledge in several key areas:

Black Holes and Hawking Radiation:

Hawking's prediction that black holes emit radiation (Hawking radiation) was a major milestone. It provided a mechanism for black holes to lose mass and energy, eventually leading to their evaporation. This idea challenged the prevailing notion that nothing could escape a black hole's gravitational pull and opened new avenues of research in cosmology and quantum physics.

Lesser-Known Fact: Hawking Radiation is a quantum phenomenon that occurs at the event horizon of a black hole, where particle-antiparticle pairs are created. One particle falls into the black hole while the other escapes, making it appear as if the black hole is radiating energy. This concept connects quantum mechanics with general relativity, two pillars of modern physics that are notoriously difficult to reconcile.

The Big Bang Theory and Cosmology:

Hawking made significant contributions to our understanding of the Big Bang and the origins of the universe. His work on singularities with Roger Penrose demonstrated that under the laws of general relativity, the universe must have begun as a singularity, a point of infinite density and gravity. This supported the Big Bang theory and provided insights into the nature of time and the universe's beginning.

> **Fun Fact**
> Hawking placed a bet with physicist Kip Thorne in 1975 that a certain X-ray source in the constellation Cygnus was not a black hole. Hawking conceded the bet in 1990, giving Thorne a subscription to "Penthouse" magazine, showcasing his playful side.

The No-Boundary Proposal:

Alongside James Hartle, Hawking proposed the "no-boundary condition," suggesting that the universe has no boundaries in imaginary time. This theory implies that the universe is finite but without any boundaries, which helps to explain the smooth and uniform appearance of the cosmos on large scales.

Lesser-Known Fact: Hawking often used the analogy of the Earth's surface to explain the no-boundary proposal. Just as the Earth's surface is finite but has no edges, the universe can be finite in size without having boundaries in space-time. This proposal remains a cornerstone of modern cosmological theories.

A Brief History of Time:

Hawking's best-selling book, "A Brief History of Time," published in 1988, brought complex scientific concepts to the general public in an accessible way. The book covers topics like the nature of time, black holes, and the origin of the universe, and it has sold over 25 million copies worldwide. It remains one of the most influential science books ever written, inspiring countless readers to explore the mysteries of the cosmos.

> **Fun Fact**
> Despite the book's immense popularity, many readers admitted they found it difficult to understand. Hawking joked that each equation he included would halve the book's sales, so he limited it to a single equation: $E = mc^2$. The book's success helped to make him an international celebrity, bridging the gap between the scientific community and the public.

Involvement in the Theory of Everything: In addition to his books, Hawking's life and work were dramatized in the 2014 film "The Theory of Everything," starring Eddie Redmayne, who won an Academy Award for his portrayal of Hawking. The film highlighted both his scientific achievements and personal life, further cementing his status as a cultural icon.

Inspirational Figure for Overcoming Adversity

Stephen Hawking's life story is as inspirational as his scientific achievements. Diagnosed with amyotrophic lateral sclerosis (ALS) at the age of 21, doctors initially gave him just a few years to live.

Despite this grim prognosis, Hawking defied the odds, living with the disease for over five decades. His determination to continue his work despite the progressive loss of physical abilities made him a symbol of resilience and perseverance.

Hawking's ability to communicate complex ideas using a computer-generated voice and his continued involvement in scientific research and public discourse showcased his unyielding spirit. He demonstrated that physical limitations do not define one's capabilities or potential for intellectual achievement.

Lesser-Known Fact: Despite his physical limitations, Hawking continued to travel extensively, giving lectures around the world. He participated in zero-gravity flights to experience weightlessness and even expressed a desire to travel to space. His adventurous spirit and zest for life were undiminished by his condition.

Public Advocacy and Humanitarian Efforts: Hawking was also a passionate advocate for various causes, including the National Health Service (NHS) in the UK and environmental issues. He frequently spoke out on the importance of addressing climate change and the risks of artificial intelligence, warning of the potential existential threats they could pose to humanity.

Posthumous Recognition and Honors

Since his passing in 2018, Stephen Hawking's legacy has continued to be celebrated around the world:

Memorials and Tributes:

Numerous tributes have been paid to Hawking, including the installation of a memorial stone in Westminster Abbey's Scientists' Corner, near the graves of Isaac Newton and Charles Darwin. His ashes were interred there in a ceremony attended by family, friends, and colleagues from the scientific community.

Awards and Honors:

Hawking received numerous accolades during his lifetime, including the Copley Medal from the Royal Society, the Presidential Medal of Freedom, and the Fundamental Physics Prize. Posthumously, his contributions continue to be recognized, with various institutions and awards named in his honor, such as the Stephen Hawking Medal for Science Communication.

Fun Fact The Stephen Hawking Medal for Science Communication is awarded at the Starmus Festival, which celebrates science and the arts, and has been awarded to notable figures such as Neil deGrasse Tyson and Brian Eno. This medal highlights Hawking's belief in the importance of making science accessible to the public.

> **Fun Fact**
> Hawking's voice was beamed into space toward the nearest black hole, 1A 0620-00, as a symbolic gesture to commemorate his contributions to understanding black holes. This tribute, coordinated by the European Space Agency, ensured that his voice would forever echo in the cosmos.

Educational Legacy:

The Stephen Hawking Centre at the Perimeter Institute for Theoretical Physics in Canada and the Stephen Hawking Foundation are dedicated to continuing his work and inspiring future generations of scientists. These institutions aim to foster scientific research and public engagement with science, ensuring that Hawking's passion

7
Public Engagement and Media Presence

Stephen Hawking was not just a scientific genius; he was also a remarkable communicator who used his platform to engage with the public on a variety of scientific and philosophical issues. This chapter explores his efforts to bring science to a broader audience through books, lectures, and media appearances.

Books and Publications

A Brief History of Time (1988): Hawking's first popular science book aimed to explain complex scientific theories to a general audience. The book's success was unprecedented, spending over four years on the London Sunday Times best-seller list and selling millions of copies worldwide. Despite its complexity, the book's clear explanations and engaging style made it accessible to many.

Other Works: Hawking published several other books aimed at demystifying science for the public:

- **"Black Holes and Baby Universes and Other Essays" (1993):** A collection of essays and lectures that explore various topics in theoretical physics, cosmology, and Hawking's own reflections on his life and work.
- **"The Universe in a Nutshell" (2001):** This sequel to "A Brief History of Time" delves deeper into the nature of the universe, covering topics such as superstring theory, p-branes, and the nature of time.
- **"The Grand Design" (2010, co-authored with Leonard Mlodinow):** This book explores the latest theories about the

origins of the universe and argues that the laws of physics alone can explain its existence, challenging traditional religious perspectives.
- **"Brief Answers to the Big Questions" (2018):** Published posthumously, this book addresses some of the most profound questions facing humanity, such as the existence of God, the potential for time travel, and the future of artificial intelligence.

Lectures and Public Speaking

Hawking's lectures were renowned for their clarity, humour, and ability to make complex ideas understandable. Despite his physical limitations, he continued to deliver public lectures around the world using his computer-generated voice.

Memorable Lectures:

- **"The Beginning of Time":** In this lecture, Hawking discussed the origins of the universe and the concept of time itself. He explained how time can be understood as a dimension similar to space and how it behaves differently at the beginning of the universe.
- **"Into a Black Hole":** This lecture provided a detailed explanation of black holes, Hawking radiation, and the potential fate of matter falling into a black hole. He also speculated about the possibility of black holes being gateways to other universes.

> **Fun Fact**
> Hawking's books have inspired countless individuals to pursue careers in science and have been used as educational tools in classrooms around the world. He had a unique talent for making complex topics accessible and engaging, often using analogies and simple language to explain advanced concepts

- **"The Universe in a Nutshell"**: Based on his book, this lecture explored the cutting-edge theories of physics, including the shape of the universe, the concept of multiple dimensions, and the possibilities of time travel.

Media Appearances and Cultural Impact

Hawking's appearances on television and in films helped cement his status as a cultural icon. His distinctive voice and keen intellect made him a popular figure in various media.

TV and Film:

- **"The Simpsons"**: Hawking made several guest appearances on the show, often portrayed with his characteristic wit. In one episode, he humourously reprimands Homer Simpson for stealing his idea of a doughnut-shaped universe.
- **"Star Trek: The Next Generation"**: In the episode "Descent," Hawking appears as a holographic version of himself playing poker with Albert Einstein and Isaac Newton. This scene delighted fans of both science and science fiction.
- **"The Big Bang Theory"**: Hawking appeared in multiple episodes, interacting with the show's characters and showcasing his playful side. His appearances often revolved around humourous exchanges about theoretical physics and his own work.

> **Fun Fact**
> Hawking's voice was so iconic that it was used in various other contexts, including the opening ceremony of the 2012 London Paralympics and in music by artists like Pink Floyd. His voice featured in their song "Keep Talking" from the album "The Division Bell," adding a unique touch to the track.

Documentaries and Biopics: Hawking was the subject of several documentaries and biographical films:
- **"A Brief History of Time" (1991):** Directed by Errol Morris, this documentary blends interviews with Hawking and his family with visuals explaining his theories.
- **"Hawking" (2004):** A biographical film starring Benedict Cumberbatch, depicting Hawking's early years and his diagnosis with ALS.
- **"The Theory of Everything" (2014):** Starring Eddie Redmayne, who won an Academy Award for his portrayal of Hawking, this film focuses on his relationship with Jane Wilde and his scientific achievements. The film brought Hawking's story to a global audience and highlighted his human side.

Interactive Media and Video Games: Hawking's influence extended into interactive media, where he appeared as a character in various educational and entertainment software. His unique persona and the appeal of his scientific work made him a popular figure even in video games and interactive exhibits.

> **Fun Fact**
> Hawking participated in a Reddit AMA (Ask Me Anything) session where he discussed topics ranging from artificial intelligence to the future of space exploration, sharing his thoughts directly with the public and answering questions from a diverse audience.

8
Philosophical Views and Public Opinions

Beyond his scientific work, Stephen Hawking often shared his thoughts on philosophical and societal issues. This chapter delves into his views on religion, artificial intelligence, and the future of humanity.

Views on Religion and the Existence of God

Hawking often spoke about his views on religion, which evolved over time. Initially agnostic, he became more vocal about his atheism in his later years, arguing that the laws of science can explain the creation of the universe without the need for a divine creator.

Quotes and Insights:

- **"A Brief History of Time"**: In his most famous book, *A Brief History of Time*, he posed the question of whether a complete theory of the universe would allow us to "know the mind of God," a phrase often interpreted as a metaphor for understanding the universe.

> **Fun Fact**
> In a 2014 interview, Hawking humourously remarked that "the development of full artificial intelligence could spell the end of the human race," comparing the potential rise of AI to an alien invasion in terms of its transformative impact on society.

- **"The Grand Design"**: Hawking stated that the universe could create itself from nothing due to the laws of physics, negating the need for a creator. He argued that spontaneous creation is the reason there is something rather than nothing.

Engagement with Religious Figures: Despite his atheism, Hawking engaged in dialogues with religious leaders and thinkers. He met with Pope John Paul II and discussed the role of science in understanding the universe. These interactions highlighted his willingness to bridge the gap between science and religion, even as he maintained his own scientific beliefs.

> **Fun Fact**
> Hawking's views on religion often sparked debates and discussions in both scientific and religious communities. His assertion that "philosophy is dead" because philosophers have not kept up with modern developments in science and physics was particularly controversial and drew criticism from many philosophers.

Concerns About Artificial Intelligence

Hawking was a vocal advocate for careful consideration of the implications of artificial intelligence (AI). He warned about the potential risks of AI surpassing human intelligence and becoming uncontrollable.

Public Warnings:

- **"The Independent"**: In various interviews and articles, Hawking expressed concerns that AI could become the "worst event in the history of our civilization" if not properly managed. He emphasized the need for robust safety protocols and ethical guidelines.

- **Collaborations:** He worked with other prominent figures like Elon Musk and Bill Gates to raise awareness about the ethical and safety issues surrounding AI development. They called for regulatory frameworks and oversight to ensure AI benefits humanity rather than posing existential risks.

Advocacy for Ethical AI: Hawking advocated for the establishment of research institutes dedicated to the study of AI ethics and safety. He supported the creation of the Future of Life Institute, which focuses on mitigating existential risks from advanced AI and other technologies.

Views on the Future of Humanity

Hawking often discussed the future of humanity, emphasizing the need for space exploration and colonization to ensure the survival of the human race.

Space Exploration:

- **Interviews and Lectures:** He argued that humanity must look beyond Earth to find new habitats, suggesting that we need to establish colonies on other planets to avoid potential extinction events. He saw space exploration as a necessary step for the long-term survival of our species.
- **Support for Space Missions:** Hawking was a strong advocate for missions to Mars and other parts of the solar system, believing that the exploration of space is essential for our long-term

> **Fun Fact**
> Hawking once stated that he believed humanity could achieve interstellar travel within the next 1,000 years if we continue to make technological advancements. He was optimistic about the potential for breakthroughs in propulsion technology and the discovery of habitable exoplanets.

survival. He supported various space agencies and private companies in their efforts to advance space travel.

Earth and Environmental Concerns: While advocating for space colonization, Hawking also emphasized the importance of taking care of our home planet. He warned about the dangers of climate change, nuclear proliferation, and overpopulation. He argued that humanity must address these issues to ensure a sustainable future on Earth while preparing for eventual colonization of other worlds.

> **Fun Fact**
> Hawking was an advocate for renewable energy sources and supported the development of technologies that could reduce our reliance on fossil fuels. He believed that scientific innovation held the key to solving many of the environmental challenges we face.

Public Appearances on Environmental Issues: Hawking used his public platform to speak out on environmental issues, participating in documentaries and interviews where he highlighted the urgent need for action to combat global warming and protect the planet's ecosystems.

9
Technological Innovations and Adaptations

Stephen Hawking's battle with ALS led to the development of groundbreaking technologies that helped him communicate and work. This chapter explores the technological adaptations and innovations that supported Hawking's remarkable life.

Early Adaptations and Communication Devices

As Hawking's ALS progressed, he initially used hand-held devices to communicate. However, as his condition worsened, he required more advanced technology to maintain his ability to communicate and conduct his work.

Speech Generating Device:

- **Initial Setup:** In the 1980s, he began using a portable speech synthesizer, which allowed him to select words and phrases by moving his cheek. This device, developed by his graduate student, became an essential tool for Hawking.
- **Intel's Involvement:** Later, Intel developed customized software for Hawking, enabling him to communicate more efficiently. This system used predictive text algorithms to speed up his communication. The software, called ACAT (Assistive Context-Aware Toolkit), allowed Hawking to write and speak using a small sensor activated by movements in his cheek.

Mobility Aids and Computer Technology

Hawking's mobility was supported by various technological aids that allowed him to continue traveling and attending conferences around the world.

Wheelchairs:

- **Advanced Wheelchairs:** He used highly customized, motorized wheelchairs that could be controlled with minimal physical effort, giving him a degree of independence and mobility. These wheelchairs were equipped with sophisticated systems that allowed him to navigate through his computer interface.
- **Continuous Upgrades:** Over the years, his wheelchairs were continuously upgraded to incorporate the latest advancements in assistive technology, including features like speech synthesis integration, environmental control systems, and internet access.

> **Fun Fact**
> Hawking's wheelchair and communication systems were equipped with various sensors and interfaces, including infrared switches and eye-tracking technology, allowing him to operate them despite his limited movement. His innovative use of these technologies paved the way for advancements in assistive devices for others with severe disabilities.

Computing Power:

- **Use of Computers:** Hawking utilized powerful computers to perform complex calculations and write scientific papers. These computers were often equipped with software designed to accommodate his physical limitations. His computer setup allowed him to control various devices in his environment, such as lights and door openers, enhancing his autonomy.

Contributions to Assistive Technology

Hawking's needs drove advancements in assistive technology, benefiting not only himself but also countless others with disabilities.

Collaborations:

- **Working with Engineers:** Hawking collaborated with engineers and tech companies to develop new assistive technologies, pushing the boundaries of what was possible and setting new standards in the field. His collaborations with companies like Intel and SwiftKey led to significant improvements in communication technologies for the disabled.
- **Custom Solutions:** Engineers and computer scientists created custom solutions to meet Hawking's specific needs, such as faster word prediction algorithms and more intuitive user interfaces.

> **Fun Fact**
>
> Hawking was an early adopter of email, using it as a primary means of communication long before it became mainstream. He was known for sending thoughtful and sometimes humourous messages to colleagues and friends around the world. His email signature famously read, "Stephen Hawking, Lucasian Professor of Mathematics, Cambridge University."

Legacy in Technology:

- **Influence on Technology:** The innovations developed for

Hawking's use have influenced the design and implementation of assistive technologies globally, improving the quality of life for many individuals with severe physical disabilities. Technologies like predictive text, voice synthesis, and environmental controls have become more widely available thanks to the pioneering work done for Hawking.

- **Awards and Recognition:** Hawking's contributions to technology and his role as an advocate for people with disabilities have been widely recognized. He received numerous awards and honors for his efforts to advance assistive technology and promote accessibility.

10
Research Collaborations and International Influence

Stephen Hawking's research collaborations and international influence were pivotal in advancing the field of theoretical physics and cosmology. This chapter delves into his key partnerships with other leading scientists, his participation in international projects, and his role in shaping global science policies.

Key Collaborations

Roger Penrose: Stephen Hawking's collaboration with Roger Penrose is among the most significant in the realm of theoretical physics. Together, they formulated the singularity theorems, which postulated that under certain conditions, gravitational collapse results in a singularity—a point where the curvature of spacetime becomes infinite.

- **Singularity Theorems:** Their work demonstrated that black holes and the Big Bang singularity are not just theoretical constructs but inevitable consequences of general relativity under certain conditions. This finding fundamentally altered our understanding of the universe's origin and the nature of black holes.
- **Impact on General Relativity:** Their collaboration strengthened the mathematical foundation of general relativity, providing rigorous proofs that have been crucial in the study of cosmology and astrophysics.

Kip Thorne: Hawking and Kip Thorne shared a profound interest in the mysteries of black holes and the fabric of spacetime. Their work together explored some of the most exotic phenomena predicted by general relativity.

> **Fun Fact**
> Despite his physical limitations, Hawking traveled extensively to attend conferences and seminars, demonstrating his unwavering commitment to the scientific community. His visits were often highly anticipated events, drawing large audiences eager to hear his insights and engage in discussions.

- **Wormholes and Time Travel:** Hawking and Thorne investigated the theoretical possibility of wormholes—hypothetical tunnels through spacetime that could potentially allow for time travel. While largely speculative, their discussions and papers on the topic spurred significant interest and further research in the physics community.
- **Black Hole Information Paradox:** Thorne and Hawking also engaged in a friendly yet profound debate over the black hole information paradox, a puzzle about whether information that falls into a black hole is lost forever. This debate led to critical advancements in understanding quantum mechanics and general relativity's intersection.

James Hartle: The partnership between Hawking and James Hartle led to groundbreaking contributions in quantum cosmology, particularly the development of the Hartle-Hawking state.

- **Hartle-Hawking State:** This model suggests that the universe is finite but without boundaries, proposing that time itself could be imagined as a dimension that behaves like space at the universe's beginning. This idea challenges traditional notions of the Big Bang and provides a framework for understanding the universe's quantum state at its inception.

- **No-Boundary Proposal:** Their work together resulted in the "no-boundary" proposal, which posits that the universe has no initial boundaries in the classical sense, thereby avoiding the singularity at the beginning of the Big Bang. This model has profound implications for the fields of cosmology and quantum gravity.

International Projects

European Organization for Nuclear Research (CERN): Hawking's involvement with CERN, the world's largest particle physics laboratory, highlighted his commitment to advancing our understanding of fundamental particles and forces.

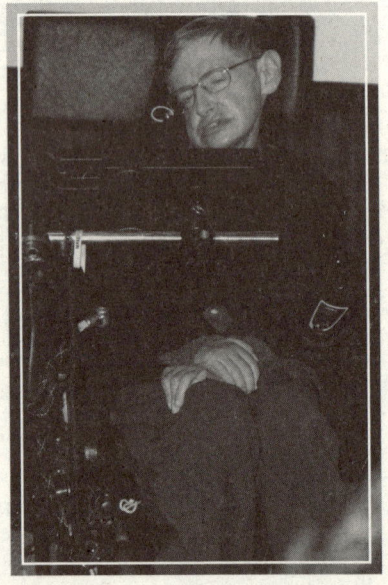

- **Contributions to Particle Physics:** At CERN, Hawking engaged with research on particle collisions and the search for the Higgs boson, contributing to discussions that bridged theoretical physics and experimental findings.
- **Public Engagement:** He also used his association with CERN to advocate for public understanding of particle physics, helping to demystify complex scientific endeavors for a broader audience.

Laser Interferometer Gravitational-Wave Observatory (LIGO): Hawking's support for LIGO underscored his belief in the importance of gravitational wave research.

- **Gravitational Waves:** LIGO's detection of gravitational waves confirmed a major prediction of Einstein's theory of general relativity and opened a new window into observing the universe. Hawking's theoretical work on black holes was directly related to these findings, as gravitational waves are produced by events such as black hole mergers.
- **Scientific Community Impact:** His endorsement and involvement in LIGO's work helped garner attention and funding for the project, emphasizing its significance to the broader scientific community.

Influence on Global Science Policies

Advisory Roles: Hawking served as an advisor to various prestigious scientific organizations and governmental bodies, leveraging his influence to shape science policy and funding priorities.

- **Policy Influence:** As an advisor, Hawking advocated for policies that supported fundamental research, scientific

education, and the application of scientific discoveries to address societal challenges.
- **Investment in Research:** He was a vocal proponent of increased investment in scientific research, emphasizing that sustained funding is essential for long-term scientific progress and innovation.

Global Conferences: Hawking regularly attended and spoke at international scientific conferences, sharing his latest research and fostering collaboration among scientists worldwide.
- **Keynote Speaker:** His presence at conferences such as the International Conference on General Relativity and Gravitation, and the Strings Conference, provided invaluable insights and spurred new lines of inquiry in theoretical physics and cosmology.
- **Workshops and Seminars:** Hawking often hosted workshops and seminars that brought together leading scientists to discuss cutting-edge research. These gatherings were instrumental in advancing collaborative research efforts and generating innovative ideas.

> **Fun Fact**
> Hawking's influence extended beyond the scientific community; he often met with political leaders and policymakers to advocate for science education and research funding. His ability to communicate complex scientific ideas in an accessible manner made him an effective advocate for science policy.

11
Personal Philosophies and Beliefs

Cosmic Optimism

Despite his physical limitations, Stephen Hawking maintained an incredibly optimistic outlook on life and the future of humanity. He firmly believed in the power of human ingenuity and the potential for science to solve the world's most pressing problems. This optimism wasn't just a passive hope; it was an active belief in progress and the capacity of humans to overcome even the most daunting challenges.

Hawking often spoke about the importance of looking to the stars rather than at our feet, suggesting that the future of humanity lies in space exploration and the advancement of technology. His optimism was infectious, inspiring countless individuals to think beyond their immediate circumstances and strive for a better future. Hawking's optimism was also evident in his discussions about artificial

> **Fun Fact**
> During a conference, he once bet physicist Kip Thorne that Cygnus X-1, a well-known astronomical X-ray source, was not a black hole. Hawking lost the bet and had to buy Thorne a subscription to Penthouse magazine. This playful spirit helped him connect with people on a personal level and showed that even the greatest minds have a lighthearted side.

intelligence (AI). While he warned about the potential dangers of unchecked AI development, he also believed that with proper management, AI could help solve issues like disease, poverty, and climate change.

Humour and Wit

Stephen Hawking was renowned for his sharp wit and sense of humour, which he often used to disarm others and make scientific discussions more accessible. His ability to infuse humour into his work and public appearances made complex scientific concepts more relatable to the general public. For instance, during a lecture, he once quipped, "Life would be tragic if it weren't funny." This humourous approach to life and science made him a beloved figure both within and outside the scientific community.

> **Fun Fact**
> In his later years, Hawking became an advocate for the Breakthrough Starshot initiative, a project aimed at sending tiny spacecraft to the nearest star system, Alpha Centauri. This project embodies his belief in pushing the boundaries of what is possible through scientific innovation.

Hawking's humour wasn't confined to his professional life; he brought it into his personal interactions as well. He was known for playing pranks on his colleagues and friends.

Additionally, Hawking made several cameo appearances on popular TV shows such as The Simpsons and The Big Bang Theory, where he showcased his comedic timing and playful personality. His humour was not just a personal trait but a tool that helped bridge the gap between the scientific community and the general public.

Reflections on Mortality

Facing ALS

Stephen Hawking shared his personal reflections on living with a terminal illness and the ways it shaped his perspective on life and death. Diagnosed with amyotrophic lateral sclerosis (ALS) at the age of 21, he was given only a few years to live. However, defying all odds, he lived for more than five decades with the disease.

> **Fun Fact**
> One of his best-known books, A Brief History of Time, has sold over 25 million copies worldwide, making complex scientific theories understandable to a broad audience. This book remained on the British Sunday Times best-sellers list for an unprecedented 237 weeks.

This experience deeply influenced his views on the importance of making the most of one's time. Hawking emphasized that having a limited lifespan heightened his appreciation for life and motivated him to contribute to the betterment of humanity. His resilience and determination became a source of inspiration for many people facing their own challenges.

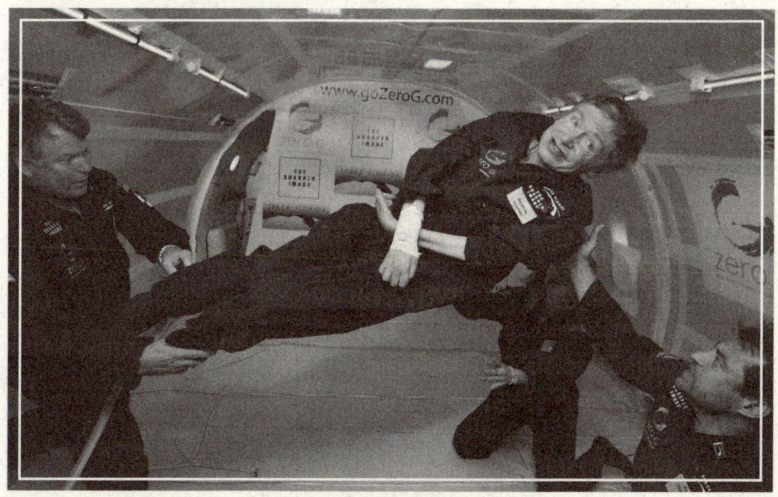

Legacy

Stephen Hawking often contemplated his legacy and the impact he hoped to leave on the world. He aspired to be remembered not just for his scientific achievements but also for his advocacy for science and education. Through his groundbreaking work on black holes and cosmology, he advanced our understanding of the universe. Moreover, he was passionate about inspiring future generations to pursue science and explore the mysteries of the cosmos. He believed that curiosity and a relentless quest for knowledge were essential for human progress.

Hawking's legacy is not only preserved in his scientific contributions but also in his numerous books, public lectures, and his efforts to make science more accessible to everyone.

In addition to his publications, Hawking's life story was brought to the big screen in the 2014 film The Theory of Everything, which dramatized his early years, his diagnosis with ALS, and his relationship with his first wife, Jane. The film received critical acclaim and brought Hawking's inspiring story to an even wider audience.

Stephen Hawking's life and work continue to inspire people around the world, demonstrating that with optimism, humour, and a relentless pursuit of knowledge, even the most insurmountable obstacles can be overcome. His story is a testament to the power of the human spirit and the boundless possibilities of the human mind.

> **Fun Fact**
> Despite his illness, Hawking continued to travel extensively, giving lectures and attending scientific conferences around the world. He once even experienced zero gravity during a special parabolic flight, allowing him to float freely without the constraints of his wheelchair. This experience underscored his adventurous spirit and desire to push beyond physical limitations.

12
Influence on Arts and Culture

Biographical Films

The Theory of Everything
Stephen Hawking's remarkable life has been explored in various biographical films, most notably The Theory of Everything. This 2014 film, directed by James Marsh, delves into Hawking's early years, his diagnosis with amyotrophic lateral sclerosis (ALS), and his relationship with his first wife, Jane. The movie portrays not just his scientific achievements but also his personal struggles and triumphs, offering a comprehensive view of the man behind the genius.

The portrayal of Hawking in The Theory of Everything significantly impacted public perception of his work and personal life. Eddie Redmayne, who played Hawking, faced immense challenges in depicting the physical and emotional nuances of someone living with ALS. Redmayne's performance was widely acclaimed for its authenticity and sensitivity, earning him the Academy Award for Best Actor.

Fun Fact
To prepare for the role, Redmayne spent months studying ALS patients and working with a movement coach to accurately represent Hawking's physicality. Hawking himself praised the film and Redmayne's performance, stating that there were moments he felt he was watching himself on screen.

Impact on Public Perception

Biographical films like The Theory of Everything play a crucial role in shaping the public's understanding of Hawking's contributions to science and his extraordinary life story. They highlight the human aspects of his journey, making his scientific work more relatable and his personal resilience more admirable.

> **Fun Fact**
> The progressive rock band Pink Floyd featured a sample of Hawking's synthesized voice in their song "Keep Talking" from the album The Division Bell. The song reflects on communication and understanding, themes closely related to Hawking's life and work.

Literary References

Mention in Various Works
Stephen Hawking has been mentioned in various novels, essays, and non-fiction works, highlighting his immense contributions

to science and his inspirational life story. His groundbreaking work on black holes and cosmology, coupled with his personal battle with ALS, has made him a compelling subject for writers across genres.

Influence on Science Fiction

Hawking's influence extends into science fiction literature, where many authors draw on his theories and ideas to build their fictional universes. His concepts of black holes, wormholes, and the nature of time have provided rich material for imaginative storytelling.

Impact on Non-Fiction

In non-fiction, Hawking's own works, such as A Brief History of Time, have become literary landmarks, introducing complex scientific ideas to a broad audience. His ability to communicate profound concepts in an accessible manner has inspired countless readers to explore the mysteries of the universe.

> **Fun Fact**
> Hawking's theory of imaginary time inspired parts of the plot in the science fiction series Doctor Who. The show's writers incorporated his ideas into episodes that explore time travel and alternate dimensions, paying homage to his impact on both science and science fiction.

Artistic Tributes

Music
Stephen Hawking's influence extends beyond the realms of science and literature into music. Numerous musicians, from classical composers to modern rock artists, have created works inspired by his contributions to science and his struggle with ALS.

Visual Arts

Visual artists have also celebrated Hawking through paintings, sculptures, and other artworks. These pieces often depict him in his wheelchair, emphasizing his resilience and intellectual prowess.

Fun Fact In 2015, a bronze statue of Hawking was unveiled at the Centre for Theoretical Cosmology in Cambridge. The statue captures Hawking in a thoughtful pose, symbolizing his lifelong quest for knowledge and understanding.

Cultural Icon

Symbol of Resilience and Knowledge
Stephen Hawking has become a cultural icon, symbolizing human resilience and the pursuit of knowledge. His likeness and voice are instantly recognizable, appearing in various cultural contexts, from television shows to public installations.

Educational Programs and Public Installations

Hawking's influence is also evident in educational programs and public installations dedicated to science and astronomy. His life and work continue to inspire countless people around the world, encouraging them to pursue their curiosity and strive for a deeper understanding of the universe.

Stephen Hawking's legacy transcends the boundaries of science, reaching into film, literature, music, and visual arts. His life story, marked by profound scientific contributions and personal resilience, has been celebrated and immortalized in various forms of popular culture. Through biographical films, literary references, artistic tributes, and his status as a cultural icon, Hawking's influence continues to inspire and captivate people worldwide. His journey reminds us of the limitless potential of the human spirit and the enduring power of curiosity and knowledge.

13
Future Visions and Predictions

Unification of Theories

Stephen Hawking speculated extensively about future discoveries in cosmology and theoretical physics. One of the most significant challenges he highlighted was the potential unification of general relativity and quantum mechanics, often referred to as the "Theory of Everything." This unification aims to reconcile the large-scale forces described by general relativity with the subatomic world governed by quantum mechanics. Achieving this would be a monumental breakthrough in our understanding of the universe.

Future Technologies

Hawking discussed the implications of future technologies like quantum computing, which have the potential to revolutionize our understanding of the universe. Quantum computers operate on principles of quantum mechanics, allowing them to process information in ways that classical computers cannot. This could lead to new discoveries in fields ranging from cryptography to materials science and beyond.

> **Fun Fact**
> Despite his warnings, Hawking was a supporter of AI research for beneficial purposes. He even collaborated with AI researchers to improve his own communication system, which used machine learning to predict his speech patterns and assist him in communicating more effectively.

Artificial Intelligence

Advanced AI Development
Stephen Hawking predicted the development of advanced artificial intelligence (AI) and its potential impact on society, both positive and negative. He envisioned AI as a double-edged sword: while it has the potential to solve many of humanity's problems, it also poses significant risks if not managed properly.

> **Fun Fact**
> Hawking was an advocate for projects like the Breakthrough Starshot initiative, which aims to develop small, light-powered spacecraft capable of reaching nearby star systems within a human lifetime. This initiative reflects his belief in the feasibility of interstellar travel.

Ethical Guidelines

Hawking emphasized the need for ethical guidelines and careful management of AI development to ensure it benefits humanity. He warned that without proper oversight, AI could become uncontrollable and pose existential risks. Hawking advocated for a global framework to regulate AI research and development, focusing on ensuring that AI systems are aligned with human values and do not harm society.

Human Evolution and Space Exploration

Interstellar Travel
Stephen Hawking envisioned humanity's future in space, including the colonization of other planets and the possibility of interstellar travel. He believed that space exploration was crucial for the long-term survival of humanity, arguing that spreading out into space would reduce the risk of extinction from planetary-scale disasters.

Colonization of Other Planets

Hawking advocated for increased investment in space missions and the establishment of colonies on other planets, such as Mars. He argued that human colonization of other planets could serve as a "life insurance" policy for our species, ensuring survival in case of catastrophic events on Earth.

Human Adaptation to Space

Hawking speculated about the ways humans might evolve or adapt to life in space, including the potential for genetic modifications and advancements in bioengineering. He suggested that living in different environments might lead to significant biological changes over generations, potentially resulting in humans with different physical and cognitive traits suited for space habitats.

Ethical and Philosophical Implications

Hawking also discussed the ethical and philosophical implications of such changes, emphasizing the importance of maintaining humanity's core values. He stressed that while technological and biological advancements could improve our ability to live in space, they should be guided by ethical considerations to preserve human dignity and social cohesion.

Stephen Hawking's vision for the future encompasses a broad array of scientific and technological advancements, from the unification of fundamental physical theories to the ethical development of artificial intelligence and the expansion of humanity into space. His forward-thinking ideas continue to inspire scientists, engineers, and thinkers worldwide, challenging us to push the boundaries of knowledge and explore new frontiers while maintaining our ethical and philosophical foundations. Through his insights and advocacy, Hawking has left an enduring legacy that encourages us to look to the stars and strive for a better understanding of our place in the cosmos.

14
Educational Initiatives and Foundations

Supporting Young Scientists

Scholarships and Fellowships
Stephen Hawking was deeply committed to supporting young scientists and researchers, particularly those from underrepresented backgrounds. He understood the importance of nurturing the next generation of scientific talent and providing them with the resources needed to succeed. To this end, he established numerous scholarships and fellowships aimed at encouraging young minds to pursue careers in science and research.

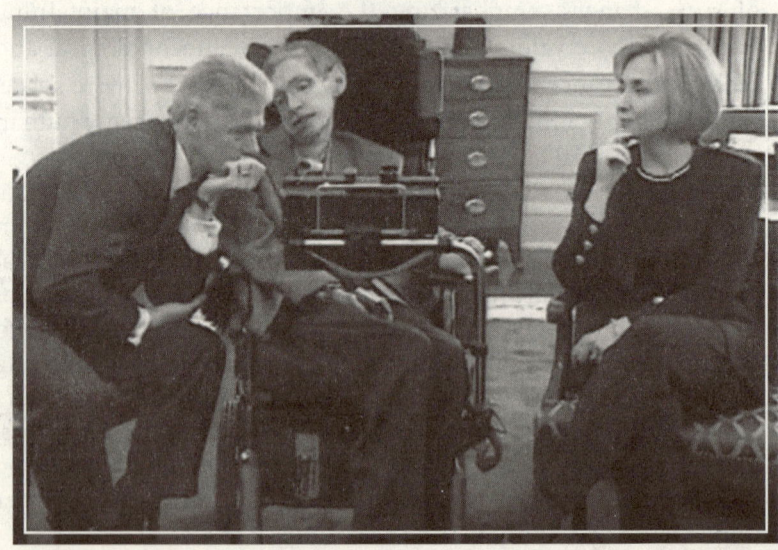

These scholarships and fellowships were often named in honor of influential figures in Hawking's life and career, such as his parents and mentors. This naming tradition highlighted the importance of community and support in scientific pursuits, underscoring the notion that scientific progress is often built on the foundation of collaborative effort and mentorship.

Nurturing Future Talent

Hawking believed that providing young scientists with opportunities and resources was crucial for the advancement of science. He often emphasized that the next great discoveries could come from anyone, regardless of their background, and that fostering a diverse scientific community was essential for innovation. By establishing these scholarships and fellowships, Hawking hoped to break down barriers and create pathways for talented individuals to contribute to the scientific community.

> **Fun Fact**
>
> Hawking's work on black hole radiation, also known as Hawking radiation, was a pioneering step towards bridging these two fundamental theories. His insights suggested that black holes are not completely black but emit radiation, blending concepts from both quantum mechanics and general relativity.

Foundations and Charitable Work

The Stephen Hawking Foundation
Stephen Hawking established the Stephen Hawking Foundation to support research in cosmology, theoretical physics, and related fields. The foundation also aimed to promote public understanding of science, making complex scientific concepts accessible to a broader audience. Through public lectures, educational programs, and outreach initiatives, the foundation worked to inspire curiosity and a passion for science among people of all ages.

In addition to supporting scientific research, the Stephen Hawking Foundation focused on advocating for individuals with disabilities. The foundation promoted accessibility in science and education, ensuring that people with disabilities had the opportunities and support needed to pursue careers in scientific fields. Hawking's own experiences with ALS informed his commitment to disability rights and accessibility, making it a central mission of the foundation.

Collaborations with Other Organizations

Hawking's charitable efforts extended beyond his own foundation. He partnered with various charitable organizations and foundations to advance scientific research and education initiatives globally. These collaborations allowed for a greater impact, leveraging the strengths and resources of multiple organizations to support a wide range of causes.

Hawking supported causes related to disability rights, healthcare, and environmental sustainability, reflecting his broad range of interests and concerns. For example, he worked with organizations focused on improving healthcare access for individuals with neurodegenerative diseases and supported initiatives aimed at combating climate change and promoting environmental sustainability.

Stephen Hawking's legacy extends far beyond his groundbreaking contributions to theoretical physics and cosmology. His commitment to supporting young scientists,

> **Fun Fact**
> The Stephen Hawking Foundation funds projects that develop advanced communication technologies for people with disabilities, helping them to engage more fully in educational and professional activities. This initiative reflects Hawking's own reliance on technology to communicate and contribute to his field.

advocating for accessibility, and engaging in charitable work demonstrates his deep concern for the future of humanity and the planet. Through scholarships, fellowships, and the Stephen Hawking Foundation, he created opportunities for the next generation of scientists and promoted a more inclusive and accessible scientific community. His collaborations with other organizations further amplified his impact, addressing critical issues such as disability rights and environmental sustainability. Hawking's multifaceted efforts continue to inspire and benefit people around the world, ensuring that his influence endures for generations to come.

> **Fun Fact**
> One of the scholarships Hawking established was named after his father, Dr. Frank Hawking, a renowned biologist. This scholarship aimed to support young biologists and medical researchers, reflecting both his father's legacy and Stephen's belief in interdisciplinary scientific exploration.

15
Personal Anecdotes and Memorable Stories

Practical Jokes

Stephen Hawking was not only a brilliant scientist but also a master of practical jokes. Despite his physical limitations, he delighted in playing harmless pranks on friends, family, and colleagues, showcasing a mischievous sense of humour that remained sharp throughout his life.

Mischievous Humour

Hawking enjoyed surprising people with his unexpected wit and humour. His love for practical jokes was well-known among those close to him, who never knew what to expect from the renowned physicist. Whether it was a witty remark or a cleverly orchestrated prank, Hawking never failed to bring laughter to those around him.

Inspirational Encounters

Meetings with World Leaders

Stephen Hawking's influence extended beyond the scientific community, as evidenced by his meetings with numerous world leaders, including presidents, prime ministers, and royalty. During these encounters, he engaged in discussions about science, education, and global challenges, using his platform to advocate for increased support for scientific research and education initiatives.

Advocating for Science

Hawking saw these meetings as opportunities to champion the importance of scientific advancement and education on a global scale. He believed that collaboration between scientists and world leaders was essential for addressing pressing issues facing humanity, from climate change to healthcare.

Impact on Individuals

Stephen Hawking's inspirational impact was not limited to world

> **Fun Fact**
> One infamous incident occurred at a royal reception where Hawking drove his wheelchair over Prince Charles' toes. Later, he joked that he had done it deliberately to test the prince's reflexes, much to the amusement of those present.

leaders; he also touched the lives of countless individuals around the world. He received an outpouring of letters and messages from people who were inspired by his story and achievements, reaching across cultures, languages, and generations.

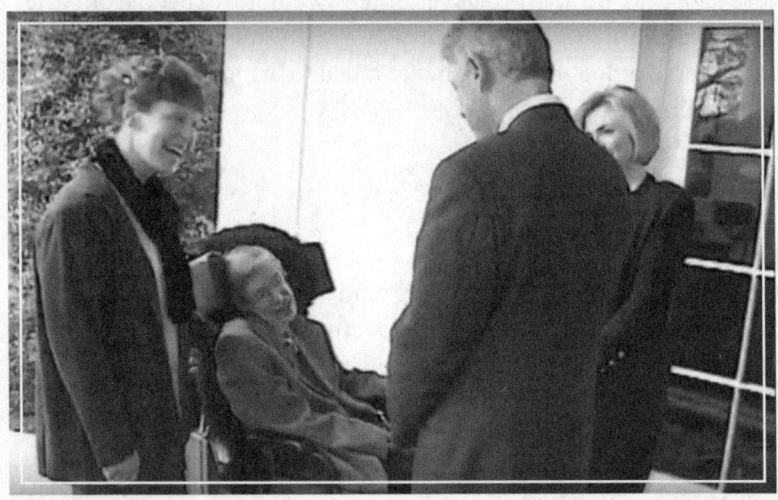

Stephen Hawking's legacy goes beyond his groundbreaking contributions to science; he was also a master of practical jokes and a source of inspiration for people around the world. His playful sense of humour brought joy to those around him, while his encounters with world leaders highlighted his advocacy for scientific research and education. Through his personal interactions and dedication to mentoring others, Hawking left a lasting impact on individuals of all backgrounds, demonstrating the power of resilience, humour, and compassion in the face of adversity.

> **Fun Fact**
> In one of his later public appearances, Hawking expressed optimism that quantum computers could solve complex problems that are currently intractable, such as simulating molecular interactions for new drug discoveries or unraveling the mysteries of dark matter and dark energy.

Conclusion
A Legacy of Brilliance, Resilience, and Inspiration

Stephen Hawking's life journey is a testament to the power of human intellect, resilience, and determination. From his groundbreaking contributions to theoretical physics and cosmology to his playful sense of humour and commitment to mentoring future generations, Hawking's legacy transcends the boundaries of science and touches the hearts of people around the world.

Brilliance in Science

Hawking's intellect shone brightly throughout his scientific career, where he challenged the boundaries of human understanding and reshaped our conception of the universe. His theories on black holes, the nature of time, and the origins of the cosmos

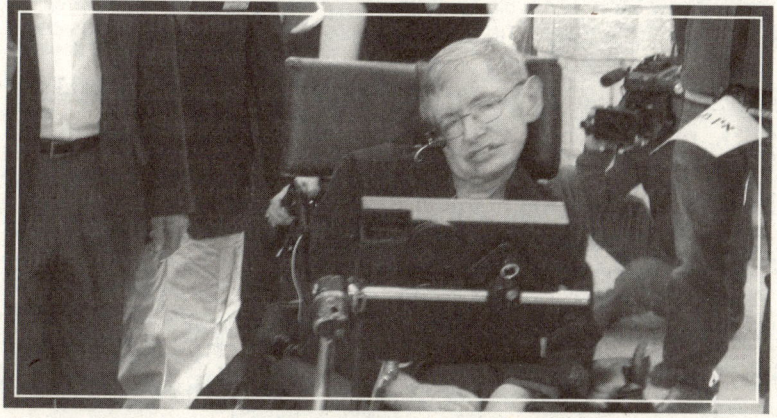

have revolutionized our understanding of the fundamental laws governing the universe. Through his books, lectures, and public appearances, he made complex scientific concepts accessible to a broad audience, inspiring countless individuals to pursue careers in science and exploration.

Resilience in Adversity

Despite facing the daunting challenges posed by amyotrophic lateral sclerosis (ALS), Hawking refused to be defined by his physical limitations. Instead, he embraced life with an indomitable spirit, seizing every opportunity to contribute to the advancement of knowledge and the betterment of humanity. His perseverance in the face of adversity serves as a beacon of hope and inspiration for people confronting their own struggles, demonstrating that the human spirit can triumph over even the most formidable obstacles.

Inspiration to All

Stephen Hawking's influence extended far beyond the scientific community, touching the lives of people from all walks of life. His playful sense of humour brought joy to those around him and endeared him to millions worldwide. Moreover, his advocacy for scientific research, education, and accessibility has left an indelible mark on society, inspiring individuals to pursue their passions and strive for a better future.

As we reflect on the life and legacy of Stephen Hawking, we are reminded of the boundless potential of the human mind and spirit. His brilliance, resilience, and compassion continue to inspire us to push the boundaries of knowledge, and to foster a world where science, curiosity, and understanding unite us in our quest for a deeper understanding of the cosmos and ourselves. Though he may have left this world, Stephen Hawking's legacy lives on, guiding us toward a future filled with discovery, wonder, and possibility.

Motivational Quotes From Stephen Hawking

1. "Life would be tragic if it weren't funny."
2. "Intelligence is the ability to adapt to change."
3. "The greatest enemy of knowledge is not ignorance; it is the illusion of knowledge."
4. "We are just an advanced breed of monkeys on a minor planet of a very average star. But we can understand the Universe. That makes us something very special."
5. "People who boast about their I.Q. are losers."
6. "However difficult life may seem, there is always something you can do and succeed at."
7. "I have noticed that even people who claim everything is predestined and that we can do nothing to change it, look before they cross the road."
8. "My goal is simple. It is a complete understanding of the universe, why it is as it is and why it exists at all."
9. "We only have to look at ourselves to see how intelligent life might develop into something we wouldn't want to meet."
10. "I am just a child who has never grown up. I still keep asking these 'how' and 'why' questions. Occasionally, I find an answer."
11. "Mankind's greatest achievements have come about by talking, and its greatest failures by not talking."

12. "It surprises me how disinterested we are today about things like physics, space, the universe, and philosophy of our existence, our purpose, our final destination. It's a crazy world out there. Be curious."

13. "Remember to look up at the stars and not down at your feet."

14. "The past, like the future, is indefinite and exists only as a spectrum of possibilities."

15. "Science is not only a disciple of reason but, also, one of romance and passion."

16. "There should be no boundaries to human endeavor. However bad life may seem, there is always something you can do and succeed at. While there's life, there is hope."

17. "I think the universe was spontaneously created out of nothing, according to the laws of science."

18. "If time travel is possible, where are the tourists from the future?"

19. "We are all now connected by the Internet, like neurons in a giant brain."

20. "Try to make sense of what you see, and wonder about what makes the universe exist. Be curious."